# AROUND THE WORLD ON EIGHTY LEGS

by Amy Gibson

illustrated by Daniel Salmieri

SCHOLASTIC PRESS / NEW YORK

For Connor, Eden, and Brynn, and
for my students at Cumberland
Elementary, wherever the world
may take you—AG

For beautiful Sophia—DS

Library of Congress Cataloging-in-Publication Data
Gibson, Amy (Amy S.)
    Around the world on eighty legs / by Amy Gibson ;
illustrated by Daniel Salmieri. — 1st ed.
        p. cm.
1. Animals—Juvenile literature.  I. Salmieri, Daniel, 1983–
II. Title.
    QL49.G533 2010
    590—dc22

                                            2009007160

ISBN 978-0-439-58755-6

10 9 8 7 6 5 4 3 2 1        11 12 13 14 15

Printed in Singapore 46
First edition, March 2011

The text was set in Geometric Slabserif.
The display text was set in P22 DaddyO.
The illustrations were done in watercolor, gouache, and
colored pencil.

Book design by Elizabeth B. Parisi and Whitney Lyle

FAR, FAR NORTH
(THE ARCTIC)

NORTH
AMERICA

FROM THE ANDES
TO THE AMAZON
(SOUTH AMERICA)

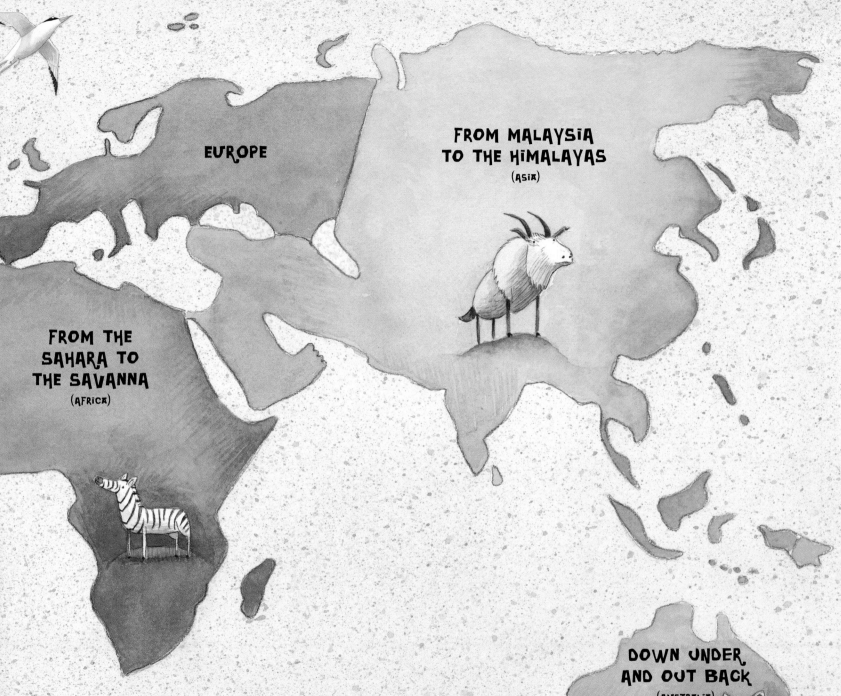

EUROPE

FROM MALAYSIA
TO THE HIMALAYAS
(ASIA)

FROM THE
SAHARA TO
THE SAVANNA
(AFRICA)

DOWN UNDER,
AND OUT BACK
(AUSTRALIA)

FAR, FAR SOUTH
(ANTARCTICA)

# FROM THE ANDES TO THE AMAZON: SOUTH AMERICA (AND BEYOND)

## HOWLER MONKEY

If camping in the Amazon,
you'll surely rise at crack of dawn.
Though little sunlight filters through,
you'll wake when howler monkeys do—

The loudest animals on land,
with voice so piercing few can stand
their eerie calls at break of day
(heard loud and clear three miles away).

The tree trunks tremble,
branches quake—

Make no mistake:
You'll be

AWAKE.

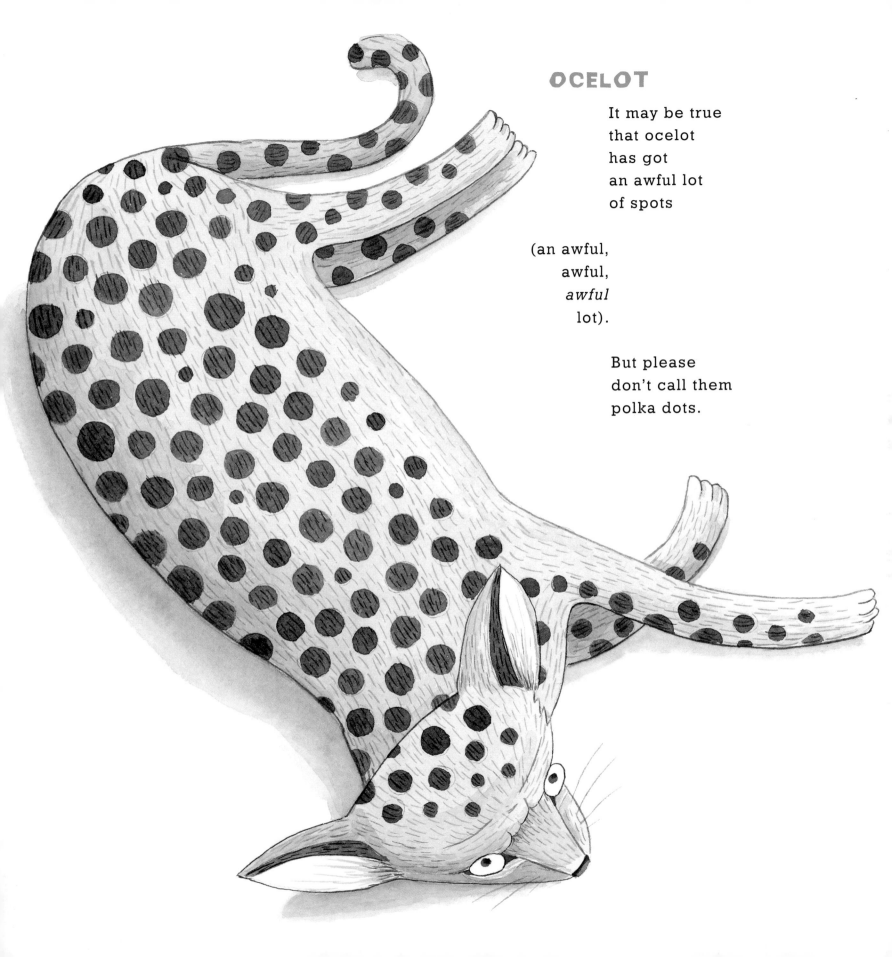

## OCELOT

It may be true
that ocelot
has got
an awful lot
of spots

(an awful,
awful,
*awful*
lot).

But please
don't call them
polka dots.

## QUETZAL

With feathers three feet long,
the quetzal's
tail could twist
into a
pretzel.

## ANACONDA

Although anaconda
is fond of
a hug,
to my liking,
his hug
is a little too snug—

And a little too strong,
and a little too long,
and that's why
when I see him,
I hurry along.

FREE
HUGS

# POISON DART FROG

In fairy tales
you kiss a frog,
and he becomes
a prince.

> The very thought
> of puckering up
> to this one
> makes me wince.

He's filled with
potent poison—
you'd drop dead
upon the spot.

> He's handsome, yes—
> bright blue and red—
> Prince Charming,
> he is *not*.

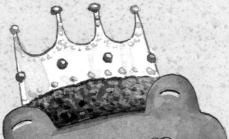

# BASILISK
(BAS-uh-lisk)

He's no wizard,
just a lizard
stuck with a
peculiar name.

What's odder,
he can walk on water!
(Just don't try
to do the same.)

## SLOTH

Day and night
in tallest trees,
sloth hangs by toes
(in twos or threes).

He slumbers
sweetly
upside down,
a hundred feet
above the ground.

When gusts of wind
come,
it's all right.
The sloth hangs
loose—
his claws hang
tight.

**PIRANHA**

Not only are his jaws ferocious, his table manners are atrocious.

## ELECTRIC EEL

In the waters
of the Amazon,
a shocking mystery's
going on—

A stunning case,
but I've a hunch
the culprit likes
*fried* fish for lunch.

Five hundred volts
to jolt his prey.
Few live to tell,
few swim away.

It's eelamentary,
dear Watson,
this one's got a
lot of
watts on.

## HOATZIN
(WAHT-zin)

If you chance
to meet a hoatzin,
you will likely flee
the spot,

for the leaves
that churn and turn
inside his stomach
reek of rot—

So you'll smell him
'fore you see him
(but you'll rather
you had not).

## AGOUTI
(uh-GOO-tee)

The agouti
gathers fruit
he finds that's
fallen to the ground.

The agouti's
solemn duty
is to scatter
it around.

For agouti
hoards his booty,
which he buries
underground.

But forgotten fruit
takes root—
that's why Brazil nut trees
abound.

## ALPACA

When hiking mountains in Peru,
up craggy peaks in blazing sun,
your Samsonite will never do.
(To lug your luggage won't be fun.)
So travel light—enjoy the view!
You suit yourself. I'll carry none.

I'll pack
an alpaca.

# CHINCHILLA

Way up high atop the Andes
(land that's mountainous
and hilly)

lives a silky silver rodent
hurrying, scurrying
willy-nilly.

When the mercury starts dropping,
does he worry?
Don't be silly!

Though it's winter,
he's so furry,
the chinchilla's not
chinchilly.

# FAR, FAR NORTH AND FAR, FAR SOUTH: THE ARCTIC AND ANTARCTIC

## CARIBOU

Through snow and sleet
one hears the beat,
the driving rain
of reindeer
feet.

The hills resound
for miles around
with wondrous,
thunderous,
tundrous
sound,
till every other noise is drowned—

For nothing mutes
like cariboots.

## ARCTIC FOX

Quiet as a whispered prayer,
by stealth she stalks the snowshoe hare
or trots behind the polar bear
    on icy Arctic floes—

    As white as snow from head to tail,
    a silent shadow, ghostly pale,
    she leaves behind a single trail
        of footprints as she goes.

## POLAR BEAR

If you'd dare
view a polar lair,
consider my advice
to you—

If polar bear
should *molars* bare,
steer clear
of his *incisors*,
too.

# AUK

When moved to talk,
the awkward auk
lets out an awful,
raucous squawk—

No dainty squeak,
no piercing shriek,
no chilling screech
slips past his beak,

no chirp, no cheep,
no happy peep,
no mournful cry
to make one weep,

no elegant trill
rolls off his bill,
no warbling tune
in octave shrill—

No, 'round the clock
the awkward auk
is doomed
to squawk
and squawk
and squawk.

## ARCTIC TERN

The migration
of the Arctic tern
is certain to
astound,

for it leaves the Arctic,
flying south
(and hardly
touches ground)

to summer on
*Antarctic* shores—

Then tern
must turn
around.

## WEDDELL SEAL

The Weddell seal's
a poor landlubber,

lumbering under
all that blubber.

But in the sea,
the joke's on you—

He's toasty warm.
*You're* turning blue.

## WALRUS

Walruses are very husky.
Walruses are very tusky.

Walruses are very clever,
using tusks just like a lever

to heave
their bodies to the ice
to bask in Arctic paradise.

# SKUA

A pirate with a scrappy streak,
the skua's got a lot of cheek—
while raiding nests,
he rarely rests,
and carries eggs off in his beak.

To put some dinner on his plate,
he steals from others. If he's late,
he'll swoop and pass,
dart, dive, harass,
and force them to regurgitate.

His calling card, his claim to fame,
is that he simply has no shame.
His attitude
is "food is food"—
fresh-caught, pre-chewed, it's all the same.

Though skua needs a talking-to
concerning manners (sad, but true),
the skua's stubborn
through and through—

It's hard to shoo a
skua.

## PENGUIN

On land, he cannot fly,
'tis true—
an awkward waddle
has to do.

But slip into the blue
below—
a tuxedoed
torpedo—

Watch him go!

## KRILL

Tiny,
briny,
run-of-the-mill,

wimpy,
shrimpy,
spineless—
still,

of creatures found
in waters chill,
none's more important
than the krill.

Krill swarm,
a massive, wriggling crowd;
they form a group
known as a cloud.

Seals gladly gulp the
pinkish horde,
this shimmering, swimming
smorgasbord.

And humpback whales
with long baleen
come sift the krill
as through a screen.

They feast (at least)
on tons a day,
a cheap, all-you-can-eat
buffet.

Oh, *everybody* wants to meet them,
*everybody* wants to eat them,
*everybody's* glad to see them—
it's just nobody wants to *be* them.

## GUILLEMOT
### (GIL-uh-mot)

Like it or not,
the guillemot
must lay eggs
in a frightful spot—

On rocky ledge,
right near the edge
(that's why each egg
looks like a wedge).

Oh, pointy eggs
sure take their toll
on Mom, when laid,
but they don't
roll.

# FROM THE SAHARA TO THE SAVANNA: AFRICA

## CAMEL

Lumpety lump
Lumpety lump
Camel resembles a
lumpety lump.
Appearing a shade
like a bed that's unmade,
he's a lumpety lumpety
lump.

Grumpety grump
Grumpety grump
Camel's a terrible
grumpety grump.
Moaning and groaning
and going "Harrumph,"
he's a grumpety grumpety
grump.

Bumpety bump
Bumpety bump
Riding one makes you go
bumpety bump.
But better to sit on
his hump
than his rump,
going bumpety bumpety
bump.

## LION

The lion is the King of Beasts—
he's mad, he's bad, he's loud.
The lion is the King of Beasts—
he's rough, he's tough, he's proud.

How does the lion use his clout
except to roll and loll about?
While lion sleeps to beat the heat,
the lioness brings home the meat.

But who eats first at lion feasts?
The lion! He's the King of Beasts!
He leaves it to the lioness
to clear the scraps, clean up the mess.

For now and then, it's quite a drain
to groom his fur, shake out his mane
(a task which proves a *royal* pain),
but he's the *King*—he can't complain.

I wonder, would things be the same
if lioness had worn the mane?

# ZEBRA

Counting zebras
isn't easy.
Counting zebras
leaves you queasy.

Counting zebras
keeps you busy.
Counting zebras
makes you dizzy.

Counting zebras
can be tricky.
Counting zebras
gets quite sticky.

Where to start?
Which one to choose?
Oh, how to tell
whose stripe is whose?

It's hard to know
how much you've got—
but safe to say,
you've got
a lot.

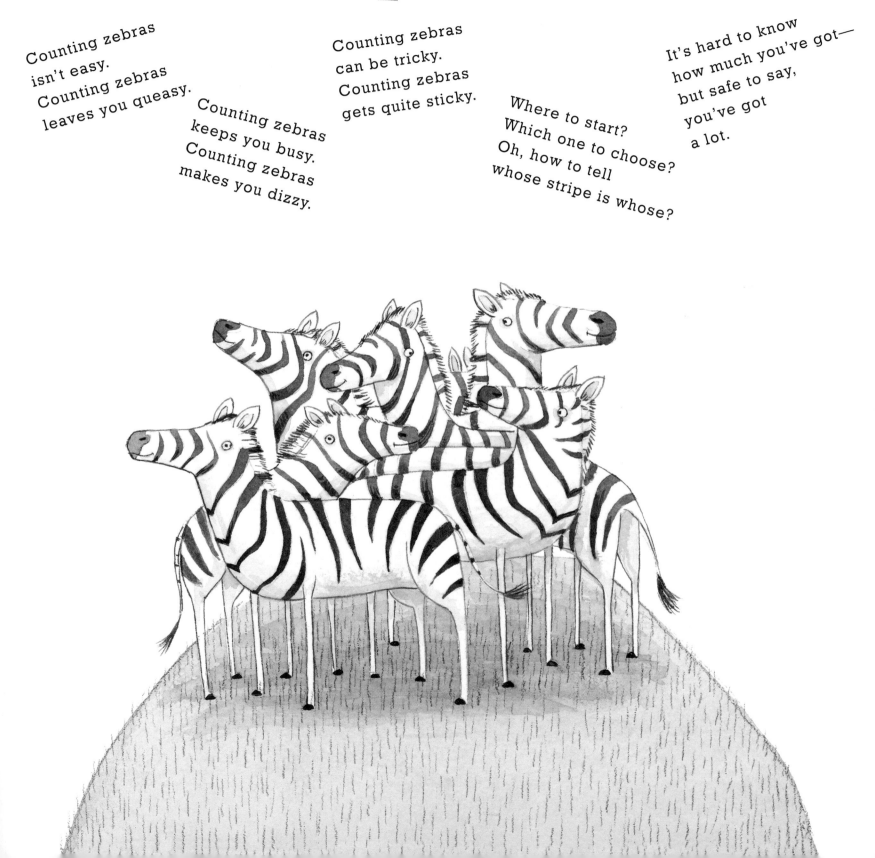

# ELEPHANT

There's nothing so grand
as an elephant band
as it toots and it trumpets
through elephant land—
    A-stamping
    and stomping,
    a-tramping
    and tromping—
The elegant elephant band.

Nobody knows
how an elephant nose
can serve as a shower,
can serve as a hose—
    A nozzle!
    A spout!
    With a spray,
    fire's out!—
The elegant elephant nose.

And who would've thunk
that an elephant trunk
could topple a tree limb
or sniff out a skunk?—
    Could daintily
    pick up
    a doughnut
    to dunk?—
The elegant elephant trunk.

Oh, the elegant elephant trunk!

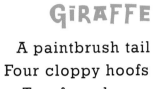

## GiRAFFE

A paintbrush tail
Four cloppy hoofs
Two furry horns
up on the roof

Four lanky legs
Four knobby knees
A foot of tongue
for grabbing leaves

A coat as gold
as honeycomb
Brown spots
like interlocking
stones

A foot or two
(oh, what the heck)
or three or four
or more of neck

Mix well. (For best results,
don't halve.)
And voilà—presto!
A giraffe.

## OSTRICH

When ostrich runs
on two-toed legs,
he speeds across
the grass.

But stretching out
his puny wings,
it's up, UP, and—
alas!

He soon outpaces
predators
no one else could
shake off.

Stunning on the runway,
he's just
shaky on the
takeoff.

## HIPPO

When hippo
wants to take a dip, oh,
how the waves
do crash and roll.

Worse yet, when hippo
wants a sip—OH,
NO! There goes
the water hole.

## CROCODILE

If you slosh through a bog,
you may find it worthwhile—

Stop and pause—

Are those jaws?
(Or a log with a smile?)

# HYENA

Oh, we smirk as we lurk
in the grass by the stream,
but we're not the bad fellows
that some make it seem.

Though we howl after hours
in a wild, eerie chorus,
and with bone-crushing jaws
we devour what's before us—

As garbage collectors
we do a great service.
(And it's not *our* fault
if we laugh
when we're nervous.)

## WARTHOG

Bless her heart,
she tries her best
but *never*
gets her beauty rest.

## RHINO

Do you suppose
the rhino grows
tired of puns
on his
rhinose?

He's got thick skin.
He doesn't mind.
It's hard to find
a thicker
rhind.

# CHEETAH

The ultimate in speed and power,
  clocked past sixty miles an hour,
    fast as lightning—
      if you ever
        want a glimpse,
          it's now or . . . . . . . . . . . . . . . . . . . . . . . . . . . . never!

# FROM MALAYSIA TO THE HIMALAYAS: ASIA

## TIGER

His roar
could shake the forest floor,
but tiger opens not his jaws—

He steals on silent, padded paws
and leaves the talking to his
claws.

## GIBBON

Watch the acrobatic gibbon
as he threads and as he weaves
through the treetops like a ribbon,
winging, swinging through the leaves—

Limb to limb
in jubilation,
hand to hand
in brachiation—

Oh, his arms are very charming
(though they hang down to his knees).

## PROBOSCIS MONKEY
(pro-BOSS-sis)

His name has been perfectly
chosen because
of his prominent, eminent,
salient schnoz.

Though his singular nose
can turn heads, without doubt,
and could rival Pinocchio's
notable snout—

Be polite. Do not stare.
Never laugh or take issue.
*Stand back* if he sneezes!
(But pass him a tissue.)

# PANGOLIN

The pangolin's
got scaly skin
from head to toe,
as hard as tin.
He rolls into
an armored ball,
and nothing,
*nothing*'s
getting in.

Without a doubt
he flaunts his snout
and waves his sticky
tongue about,
so passing ants
have not a chance,
'cause nothing,
*nothing*'s
getting out.

# ORANGUTAN

While capuchins and chimpanzees,
baboons and gibbons shoot the breeze,
orangutan keeps silent watch
upon his leafy throne.

Above the crowd, above the fray,
where vines and branches bend and sway,
orangutan, the old man of the forest,
lives alone.

His face is grizzled, wrinkled, wise.
He looks about through old man's eyes—
just what he sees, nobody knows,
although one can suppose

he visits distant memories
and sighs and weighs the fate of trees
and dreams of days of long ago,
and dreams of days of long ago.

# MOUSE DEER

Mouse deer
Mouse deer
In your forest
house deer
Eensy weensy
eeny weeny
tiny as a louse deer

Shy deer
Shy deer
Wouldn't hurt
a fly deer
Rarely stop
and say hello
before you say
good-bye deer

Hush deer
Hush deer
Tiptoe through
the brush deer
Creeping, creeping
in the night when
all is still
and shushed deer

Mouse deer
Mouse deer
Dear little
mouse deer
Itty little
bitty little
pretty little
mouse deer.

## SLOW LORiS

Loris moves so slowly, slowly
Creeping, creeping, creeping, creeping
Loris moves so slowly, slowly
While the forest's sleeping, sleeping

Loris moves so slowly, slowly
(Enemies will not detect him)
Loris moves so slowly, slowly
(Bugs he eats will not suspect him)

Loris moves so slowly, slowly
 Toe by toe by toe by toe
  He inches, inches down the row—
   So slow, so slow, so slow, so slow.

# YAK

The yakkity yakkity yakkity yak—
Why is it the yak never answers you back?
To a yak, nothing's worse
than to have to converse—
The yakkity yakkity yak.

The yakkity yakkity yakkity yak—
While little birds chirp on his backity back,
the taciturn fellow
won't let out a bellow—
The yakkity yakkity yak.

The yakkity yakkity yakkity yak—
For small talk and chitchat he hasn't the knack.
*He*'s hardly to blame—
his unfortunate name
is the yakkity yakkity yak.

Oh, the yakkity yakkity yak!

# SNOW LEOPARD

The shy snow leopard's
hard to spot—
he's seldom seen,
and seldom caught—
and camouflaged against
the snow,
he's hidden oftener
than not.

The sly snow leopard
wears a shroud
of silver mist
or wisp of cloud,
and no one hears him
come or go—
his padded paws
aren't very loud.

The high snow leopard
slips through snow—
sheer cliffs above,
sheer drops below—
on velvet paws,
on velvet toes.
Oh, why, snow leopard,
must you go?

# MACAQUE
### (muh-KAK)

Most monkeys
like it hot, but not
the Japanese
macaque.

He lives in snow
where cold winds blow,
for fur runs
down his back.

But coats of fluff
are not enough
when winter is
a doozy.

And so he hurries
when it flurries
into the
Jacuzzi.

# TAKIN
(TAH-kin)

On Himalayan mountains steep,
is it an ox?
A deer?
A sheep?

A buffalo?
Or (just for fun)
a goat
and moose
wrapped up in one?

You'll have to guess
(just do your best)—

The takin
isn't
talkin'.

# TAPIR

Though tapir's
got a funny shape,
his trunk-like snout
helps him escape.

I'd never trade
his looks for *mine*,
but tapir's suit
suits *him* just fine.

When threatened,
in the pond he goes—
submerged, all but
his snorkel nose.

To predators,
it isn't clear
if tapir's there,
or tapir's here.

Though tapir's
got a funny hide
(dark at both ends,
with white inside),

# DOWN UNDER AND OUT BACK: WHERE OTHER THAN AUSTRALIA?

## KANGAROO

Why hug the ground, when you can bound?

## JOEY

If he rode on Mom's back,
he'd receive a stiff whack
from low trees which whiz by
in a blur—

But slouched in a pouch,
joey rarely says "Ouch,"
nestled snug on a couch
made of fur.

# CASSOWARY

Nary
a cassowary
has a head that's very
hairy.

Nary
a cassowary
has a haircut
fit to see.

Nary
a cassowary
spends a moment
being wary.

For nary
a cassowary's
scared to run
into a tree.

## SUGAR GLIDER

His skin drapes
like a cape
as he makes
his escape,
and he leaps off the edge
of the tallest of trees.

Without wires
or strings
(never fear,
he's got wings!)—
he's a daredevil act
on the flying trapeze.

## BILBY

Some people say the bilby,
frankly, looks a little silly.
Is he mouse or is he rabbit?
I confess it's hard to tell.

Though he may look kind of funny,
like a rat-tailed Easter bunny,
keep your chuckling to a whisper,
for he *hears* extremely well.

# AUSTRALIAN DESERT FROG

January to December
this Australian frog
is found

burrowed deep beneath
the clay,
sleeping soundly
underground.

When raindrops
patter on his roof,
he's wakened
by the din:

Just once a year
he gets a drink—
*today*,
he's sleeping in.

# THORNY DEVIL

The prickly
thorns
upon its nose
are its sole
resemblance
to the
rose.

## EMU

Mr. and Mrs. Emu
are a liberated pair.
As husbands go, he's quite a find,
you may say, quite a catch.

For, emus two, they share the view
it's really only fair
that *he's* the one who's left to mind
the eggs until they hatch.

## KOALA

Up in silvery leaves,
lost in silvery dreams,
the koala just moseys
along.

He feels rather snoozy,
perhaps a touch woozy—

(That last eucalyptus leaf
*was* a bit strong.)

## ECHIDNA
(ih-KID-nuh)

Pointy, poky.
Prickly, stickly.
Poor echidna's
Not for tickling.

Not for holding.
Not for sitting
side by side with.
I'm not *kidding*.

## GOANNA

I'm not afraid of
the goanna.
It's just an eight-foot-long
iguana.

I'd catch one—

But I just don't
wanna.

## DINGO

An Aussie farmer
had a dog,
and dingo
was his name-o.

The flock of sheep
he liked to keep
was never quite
the same-o.

He wasn't dense.
He built a fence
through hard and heavy
labor—

A dog that's penned
is man's best friend.
(Good fences
make good neighbors.)

# OUTBACK

If you ever take a trip
across the outback
in a Jeep—

Passing sheep,
after sheep,
after sheep,
after sheep—

Be careful not to
count them,
so you don't fall
asleep.

# MENAGERIE OF FACTS

 **Agoutis** (uh-GOO-tees) are accidental gardeners. When they forget where they've buried their fruit, they plant trees by mistake.

 **Alpacas** can carry heavy loads at high altitudes. They're also raised for their cashmere-soft hair, once worn only by Incan royalty.

 If an **anaconda** wants to hug *you*, no need to feel flattered. Anacondas squeeze the life out of their prey before swallowing it whole.

 In its snow-white winter coat, the **Arctic fox** goes almost unnoticed. When galloping, its back paws follow in the hollows its front paws left behind, leaving a curious set of prints.

 No bird goes to greater lengths to avoid winter than the **Arctic tern**—more than 20,000 miles round-trip, pole to pole, in search of summer. It lives its life in almost constant daylight.

 Though they live in opposite hemispheres and are not related, **auks** resemble penguins. Awkward on land, they're amazingly graceful in water.

 When it rains, **Australian desert frogs** store water in their bodies and burrow, wrapping themselves in transparent cocoons. Then they sleep until it rains again, which may take years.

 With fringed toes and a long tail for balance, the **basilisk** (BAS-uh-lisk) can run across the surface of water. But if it slows down, it's sink or swim.

 Many Australians love **bilbies**, or rabbit-eared bandicoots. Some Australians are working to save their population—even selling chocolate Easter bilbies to raise funds.

 A **camel**'s hump is like a backpack, storing fat its body can later turn into food and water. As long as it has plants to eat, it can go months without a drink.

 **Caribou**, or reindeer, migrate in huge herds across the tundra. A line of caribou may stretch more than 180 miles.

 **Cassowaries** come equipped with crash helmets. Bony crests protect their heads when they run through the rain forest.

 No animal runs faster than the **cheetah**. But cheetahs can't keep it up for long, so they must catch dinner quickly. After sprinting, cheetahs may need half an hour to catch their breath.

 Though too modest to admit it, the **chinchilla** has the softest fur in the world—perfect for bitter cold winters.

 With only their eyes and nostrils above water, **crocodiles** lie in wait by the riverbank. Any resemblance to logs ends once they open their mouths.

 **Dingoes** are wild dogs that hunt in packs. They caused such trouble for sheep ranchers, the Australian government built a 3,400-mile-long "Dog Fence" to keep them out.

 The **echidna** (ih-KID-nuh) is a spiny anteater. When threatened, it rolls into a ball or digs into the soil, leaving its spines exposed. Predators think twice about taking a bite.

 The **electric eel**'s muscles work like batteries to generate and store electricity, which it uses to stun its prey.

 An **elephant**'s trunk is used for trumpeting, smelling, showering, breathing, wrestling, and saying hello. Baby elephants even suck them like thumbs.

 The male **emu** deserves a card on Father's Day. Unlike most birds, he's "Mr. Mom," warming the eggs and then caring for the chicks for over a year.

 **Gibbons** move by brachiation (BRAKE-ee-A-shun), swinging arm over arm. With powerful, flexible shoulders, they can even hang by one arm and swivel around.

 At eighteen feet tall—half of that its neck—a **giraffe** could look in your upstairs window. It plucks leaves from thorny acacia treetops with its long, strong tongue.

There's no shame in keeping your distance from a **goanna**, or monitor lizard. Its sharp teeth, claws, and lashing tail command respect.

Thank goodness **guillemot** (GIL-uh-mot) eggs look so funny. Their conical shape makes them roll around in a circle rather than off of the cliffs where females lay them.

Weighing up to 4.5 tons, there's nothing dainty about a **hippopotamus**. Hippos lie in the shallows by day. At sundown, they march out to the grass to eat and eat and eat.

Poor **hoatzin** (WAHT-zin or waht-SEEN)! It looks funny and smells worse. No wonder—it eats leaves that rot in its stomach and smell like cow dung.

**Howler monkeys**' extra-large voice boxes and inflatable flaps of skin amplify their calls, like megaphones. Troops howl to warn others to stay off their turf.

**Hyenas** come out at night to eat others' leftovers or hunt in packs. Their whooping calls sound like hysterical laughter but merely urge others to dinner.

The **joey**, a baby kangaroo, is born blind and helpless, the size of a grape. In its mother's pouch, it drinks milk and grows till it's too big to fit—enjoying door-to-door taxi service.

**Kangaroos** can't walk. But when they bound, they don't mess around. Red kangaroos, the largest ones, could leap over three parked cars.

**Koalas** eat only eucalyptus leaves, which smell minty like cough drops. Scientists once thought the leaves made them drowsy. They now think the leaves provide so little energy that koalas need to sleep—a lot.

**Krill** are on everyone's menu. Fortunately, there are billions of krill in the sea—enough to go around.

Of all the big cats, only **lions** live in family groups. The lion protects the pride, but the lionesses do everything else. No one works too hard—lions do a lot of lying around.

Most monkeys live in the tropics, but not the furry **macaques** (muh-KAKS), or snow monkeys, of northern Japan. To keep warm, they hop into volcanic hot springs—their very own hot tubs.

**Mouse deer** are gentle, timid creatures not much bigger than rabbits. On their delicate, pencil-thin legs, they slip through the undergrowth.

While a spotted coat stands out at a party, it helps the **ocelot** blend into the light and shadow of the rain forest.

*Orangutan* means "man of the forest." With its wrinkles and gray beard, it looks the part. Most primates live in troops, but orangutans nest alone in treetops, rarely coming down.

**Ostriches** are too plain heavy to fly. Who needs to, when you can outrun a racehorse? They've got two toes on each foot instead of four, for faster sprinting.

The **outback** is the hot, dry interior of Australia. Vegetation is sparse, so ranchers need many acres to feed their sheep. Ranches, often called stations, may stretch for miles.

The **pangolin** looks like a kind of anteater covered with overlapping scales. Curled up in a ball for protection, it resembles an overgrown pinecone.

With wings like flippers and tails like rudders, **penguins** "fly" underwater. Streamlined and speedy, they spin and twirl like acrobats.

The **piranha**'s deadly reputation is a blend of fact and fiction. Some *can* reduce an injured animal to bones in minutes. But some are vegetarian.

All **poison dart frogs** are colorful. Some are deadly. One frog's poison—the deadliest animal toxin on Earth—is used to tip blowgun darts. Kissing is definitely out.

Don't mess with a **polar bear**. A male can weigh as much as ten adult humans. On its hind legs, it wouldn't fit through your front door.

It's not hard to guess how this monkey got its name. *Proboscis* (pro-BOSS-sis) means "nose." It works like a loudspeaker to make his honking calls louder.

The ancient Maya and Aztecs prized the **quetzal** as sacred, using the feathers of this bird in headdresses.

**Rhinoceros** skin is so thick, not even a lion's claws can tear it. But even that protective hide needs protecting—rhino mud baths serve as sunscreen and insect repellent.

**Skuas** won't win any popularity contests with their neighbors. They'll hunt or eat *anything*, even food that's already been chewed.

Both two- and three-toed **sloths** do everything in s-l-o-w motion. They even *digest* slowly, coming down from their trees only every week or two to go to the bathroom.

The **slow loris** blends in with the woodwork. It hunts insects at night, moving down a branch one foot at a time, so slowly that predators don't notice it's there.

It's hard to catch a glimpse of a **snow leopard**. Even if they weren't endangered, they're shy, solitary animals. They hunt at night, high in the Himalayas.

The **sugar glider** has flaps of skin from its wrists to its ankles. They stretch like a parachute when it leaps, sailing the length of a football field in search of sugary sap.

The **takin** (TAH-kin) looks a *little* like a lot of creatures but a *lot* like none. Takins migrate through bamboo forests, sharing this habitat with pandas.

The **tapir**'s hide lets it hide in plain sight, breaking up its outline in forest light and shadow. If scared, it may duck underwater, using its snout like a snorkel to breathe.

The **thorny devil** won't be winning any beauty contests. Fortunately, those thorns make the lizard an unattractive meal for predators.

The **tiger** is the largest big cat, but not the loudest. By stealth it stalks prey through the brush, then pounces, striking a blow with its powerful paw.

Weighing as much as a car, a **walrus** can use a boost out of the water. Conveniently, both males and females come with mighty tusks, their built-in tools.

No amount of sleep will help the **warthog**'s looks. Thankfully, the wart-like growths protect its face when it charges at predators or other warthogs.

**Weddell seals** spend lots of time beneath the ice, diving over 2,000 feet and holding their breath for over an hour. They look like they're smiling. Perhaps they are. . . .

The **yak** can live at altitudes of 20,000 feet. Few animals could survive such bitter cold, but the yak manages nicely, with a thick coat that hangs to the ground.

Like fingerprints, no two **zebras**' stripes are alike, which helps zebras find each other. Stripes also work like team uniforms, making it harder for predators to pick out just one.